SAUDI ARABIA

Abby Anderson

Lerner Publications Company • Minneapolis

Lerner Publications Company
A division of Lerner Publishing Group, Inc.
241 First Avenue North
Minneapolis, MN 55401 U.S.A.

Website address: www.lernerbooks.com

Library of Congress Cataloging-in-Publication Data

Anderson, Abby.
    Saudi Arabia / by Abby Anderson.
        p.   cm. — (Country explorers)
    Includes index.
    ISBN 978–1–58013–595–5 (lib. bdg. : alk. paper)
    1. Saudi Arabia—Juvenile literature. I. Title.
DS204.25.A532 2009
953.8—dc22   2008008723

Manufactured in the United States of America
1 2 3 4 5 6 – PA – 14 13 12 11 10 09

Table of Contents

Welcome!

We're visiting Saudi Arabia! This country is in the Middle East. The Middle East is the part of Asia that meets Africa and Europe.

The Red Sea lies west of Saudi Arabia. To the north are Jordan and Iraq. Kuwait sits to the east. So do the Persian Gulf, Qatar, and the United Arab Emirates. Oman and Yemen are to the south.

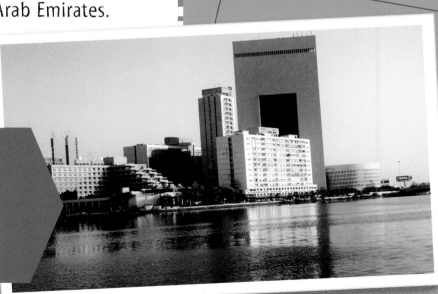

Saudi Arabia is on the Arabian Peninsula. A peninsula is a piece of land with water on three sides. The Red Sea (*right*) laps the Arabian Peninsula.

Across the Country

Much of Saudi Arabia is desert—but not all of it. The Hejaz region runs along the Red Sea's coast. Beaches and cliffs rise to hills and mountains.

The Asir region is south of Hejaz. Mountains and farmland lie there.

Farm fields cover the land in the Asir region.

Large, rocky plateaus stretch to the east. This area is called the Nejd. Lush oases dot the Nejd. Oases are moist places in a desert.

North of the Nejd is al-Nafud Desert. This desert has reddish sand dunes.

Map Whiz Quiz

Check out the map on page 5. A map is a drawing or chart of a place. Trace the map onto a sheet of paper. See if you can find the Red Sea. Color it red, and mark it with a *W* for west. Now see if you can find the Persian Gulf. Color it blue, and mark it with an *E* for East.

Crops grow at this oasis in the Nejd.

7

Deserts and Oil

A desert called Rub al-Khali lies in the southeast. It's the biggest sandy desert in the world! It's also the hottest and driest place on Earth. Temperatures can reach 120°F (49°C).

The Rub al-Khali Desert gets extremely hot in summer months. This desert is almost as big as Texas!

Sand and gravel plains border the Persian
Gulf. This dry land is called al-Hasa. Oil lies
beneath al-Hasa. People drill wells to bring
the oil to the surface.

People send oil from
al-Hasa to this
factory at the
edge of the desert.
People use the oil to
make gasoline.

9

Family Life

Saudi families are very close. Kids often live near grandparents, aunts, uncles, and cousins. The family might get together once a week.

A family enjoys a day at the beach in Saudi Arabia.

Family Words

Saudi Arabian families speak Arabic. Here are the Arabic names for family members.

grandfather	jeddee	(ZHED-ee)
grandmother	jeddatee	(ZHED-ah-tee)
father	eb	(EHB)
mother	omun	(OH-moon)
uncle	omi	(AAHM-ee)
aunt	omti	(AAHM-tee)
brother	okh	(OAK)
sister	okht	(OH-kit)
son	wuld	(WILD)
daughter	bent	(BINT)

Most Saudi Arabian women raise children and run the house. Men usually go to work and do the shopping. In modern times, some women may also have careers. But most do not. Women typically stay close to home.

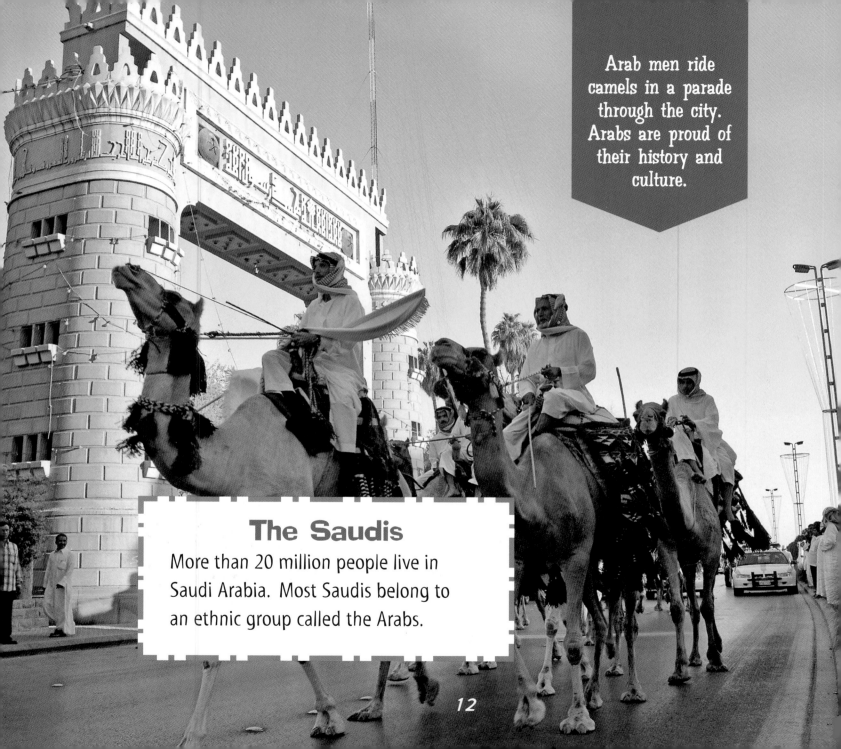

Arab men ride camels in a parade through the city. Arabs are proud of their history and culture.

The Saudis

More than 20 million people live in Saudi Arabia. Most Saudis belong to an ethnic group called the Arabs.

Arabs are linked by their language and
their history. They have lived in the area
for thousands of years.

This boy lives in a
village that is hundreds
of years old.

Desert Nomads

Some Saudi Arabian Arabs are nomads. Nomads are people who move from place to place.

Saudi nomads herd goats and sheep. They camp in tents made from goat or camel hair.

Saudi nomads camp with their camel herds in the desert.

14

Most modern-day nomads stay near hospitals and schools. That way, kids can go to classes and sick people can get treatment.

Visitors to a Saudi nomad camp share a meal.

Jidda is a large city in Saudia Arabia.

City Saudis

Most Saudi Arabians live in cities. Modern cities have schools, hospitals, roads, and malls. Gardens with fountains and pools of water dot the cities.

City dwellers live in houses or apartments with two living rooms. One is for men, and the other is for women.

Saudi men drink coffee in a living room set aside for them.

Religion

Islam is the religion of Saudi Arabia. All Saudi Arabians follow Islam. People who follow Islam are called Muslims.

Muslims visit an Islamic place of worship.

Muslims believe in one God, called Allah. They believe a prophet named Muhammad received Allah's messages. The messages became the Quran (the Islamic holy book). Kids celebrate the first time they read the Quran.

A Sacred Time

Ramadan is a sacred time for Muslims. Ramadan is the Islamic holy month. Muslims fast from dawn to sunset during Ramadan. That means they do not eat or drink. After dark, they pray at a mosque (an Islamic place of worship). Then they eat a big meal.

A schoolgirl reads from the Quran.

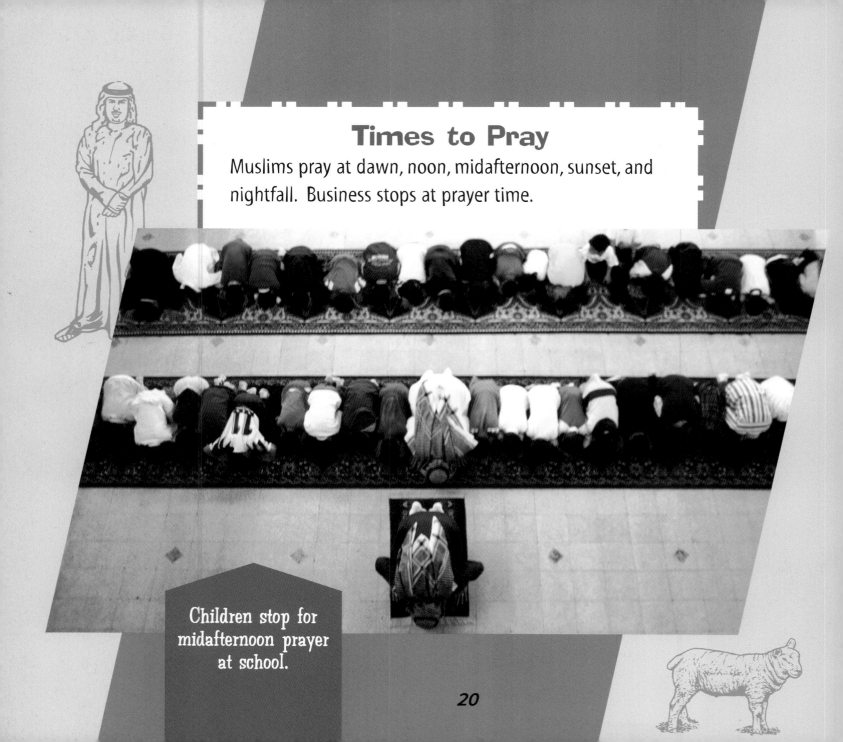

Times to Pray

Muslims pray at dawn, noon, midafternoon, sunset, and nightfall. Business stops at prayer time.

Children stop for midafternoon prayer at school.

Before praying, Muslims wash themselves. They face Mecca. That's a city in western Saudi Arabia. Muhammad was born in Mecca. It's the holiest city of Islam.

Crowds of people pray at a mosque in Mecca. All Muslims try to visit Mecca at least once.

Cover Up!

Many Saudis wear traditional clothing. Men wear a long shirt called a *thobe*. It goes all the way to the ground. They may also cover their heads with a square of cotton cloth. A black cord holds the cloth in place.

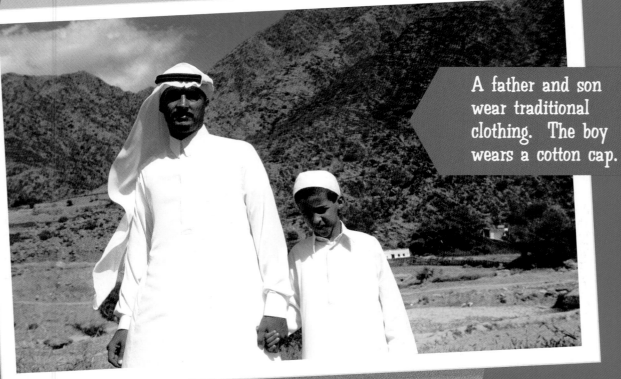

A father and son wear traditional clothing. The boy wears a cotton cap.

Women may wear jeans and casual tops at home. But in public, they wear a robe called an abaya. The abaya goes over a woman's clothes. It covers her whole body.

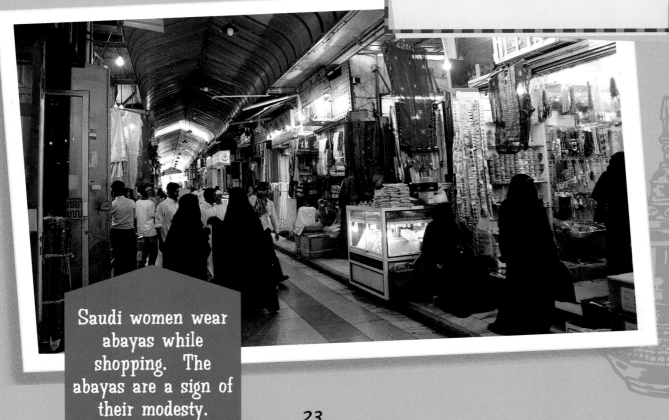

Saudi women wear abayas while shopping. The abayas are a sign of their modesty.

Kid Life

A family's love surrounds a Saudi child. Families help kids decide what to study at school, what kind of job to have, and whom to marry.

A Saudi family enjoys a ride at a fair.

Kids respect their older relatives. Children listen to older people and follow their advice.

A Saudi father plays with his daughters. They live in a nomad camp.

25

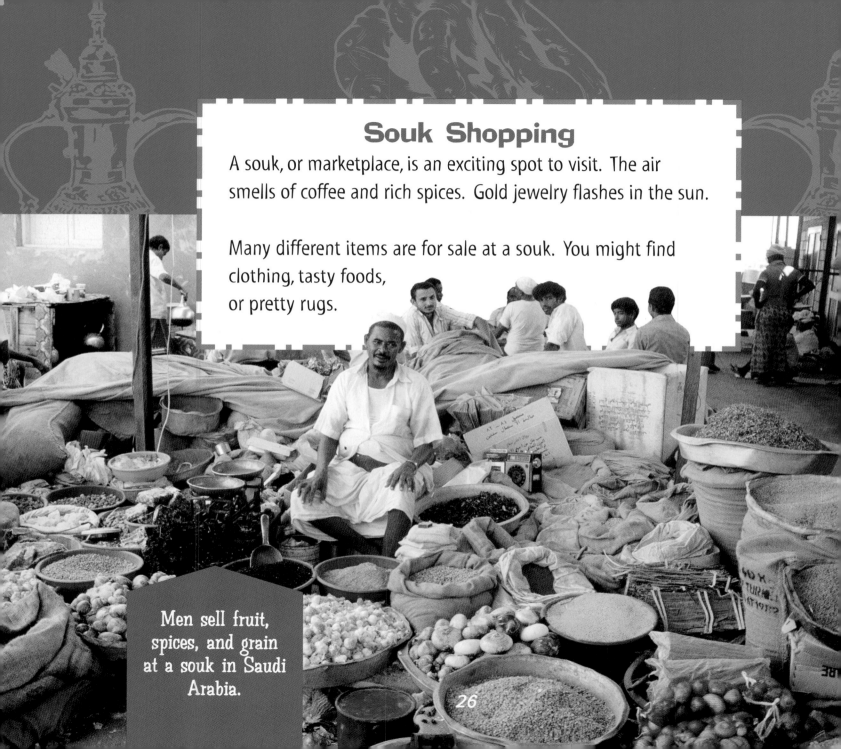

Souk Shopping

A souk, or marketplace, is an exciting spot to visit. The air smells of coffee and rich spices. Gold jewelry flashes in the sun.

Many different items are for sale at a souk. You might find clothing, tasty foods, or pretty rugs.

Men sell fruit, spices, and grain at a souk in Saudi Arabia.

26

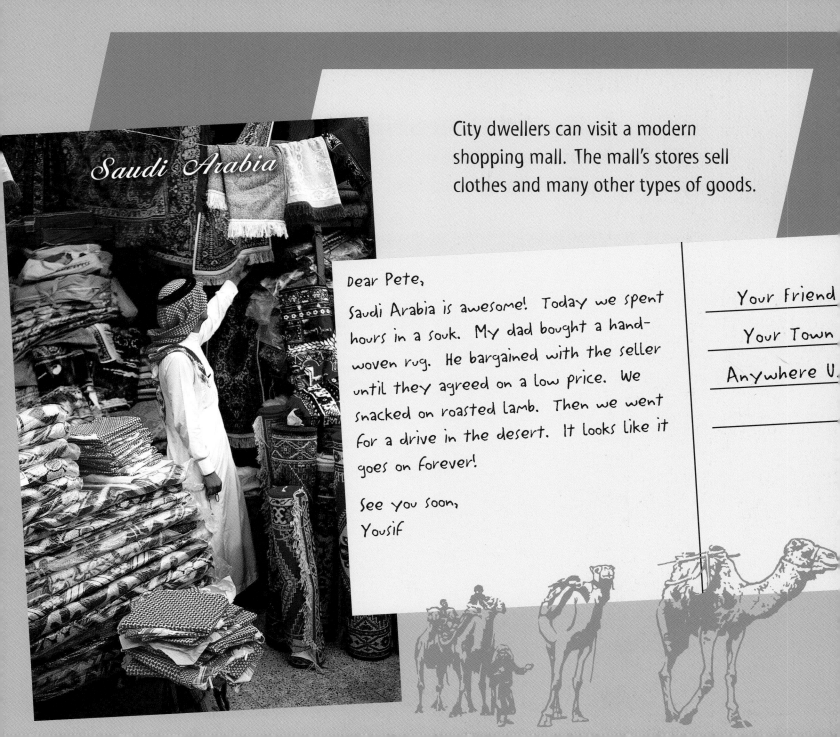

City dwellers can visit a modern shopping mall. The mall's stores sell clothes and many other types of goods.

Dear Pete,

Saudi Arabia is awesome! Today we spent hours in a souk. My dad bought a hand-woven rug. He bargained with the seller until they agreed on a low price. We snacked on roasted lamb. Then we went for a drive in the desert. It looks like it goes on forever!

See you soon,
Yousif

Your Friend

Your Town

Anywhere U.

Arabic ABCs

Arabic is the language of Saudi Arabia. The Arabic alphabet doesn't look like the alphabet that English speakers know.

These books and pages show Arabic writing.

People write Arabic from right to left. Readers turn book pages from left to right. That's opposite from the way people read books written in English. But to Saudi Arabians, English-language books look backward!

An artist uses a cut reed to write in Arabic. Most Saudis use pens or pencils to write.

Poems and Stories

Saudis love poetry! They chant it, write it, and read it.

A Saudi mother reads old stories to her daughter.

Many Saudis enjoy poems about brave people and daring deeds. Some Saudis enjoy folktales about animals. Stories of magic and wild adventures are popular too.

Saudi men clap along with folk musicians.

Time for School

Saudi boys and girls don't go to school together. Instead, they study in separate buildings.

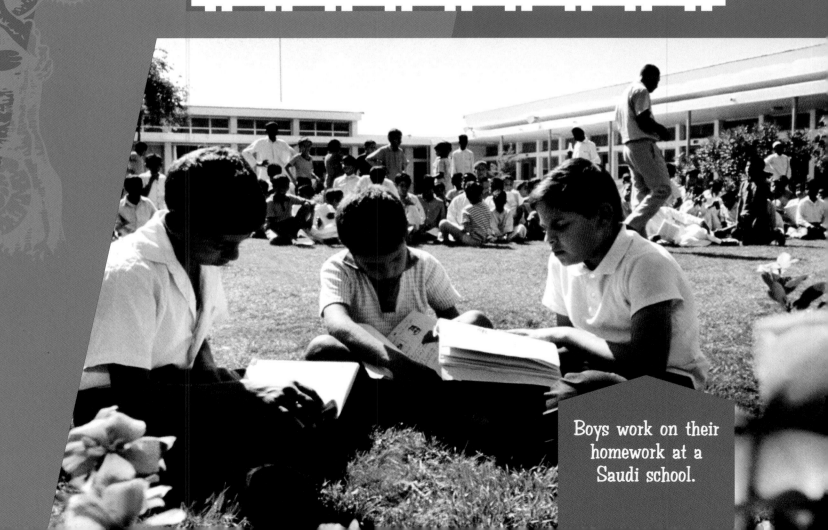

Boys work on their homework at a Saudi school.

Kids might learn math, Arabic, history, and science. Some students go on to earn college degrees.

College students study in the school library.

Big Lunch!

Lunch is the biggest meal of the day in Saudi Arabia. Saudis might eat lettuce, cucumbers, tomatoes, rice, and lamb stew.

Mint and lemon season many dishes. A flat bread called pita is served at every meal.

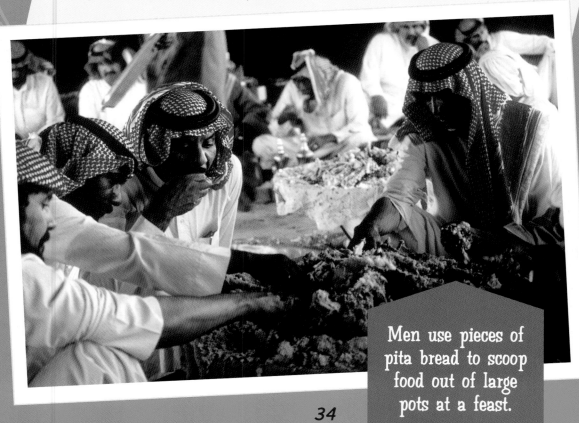

34

Men use pieces of pita bread to scoop food out of large pots at a feast.

After lunch, many people rest for a few hours. It's too hot to do much else this time of day! Kids who don't want to nap may read or do their homework.

Coffee Break

Serving tiny cups of coffee is a Saudi tradition. The host serves the oldest or most important person first. Saudis consider it polite to drink two cups but not three! To refuse the third serving, a Saudi waggles the cup back and forth.

A man pours tea for a guest. In some parts of Saudi Arabia, people prefer tea to coffee.

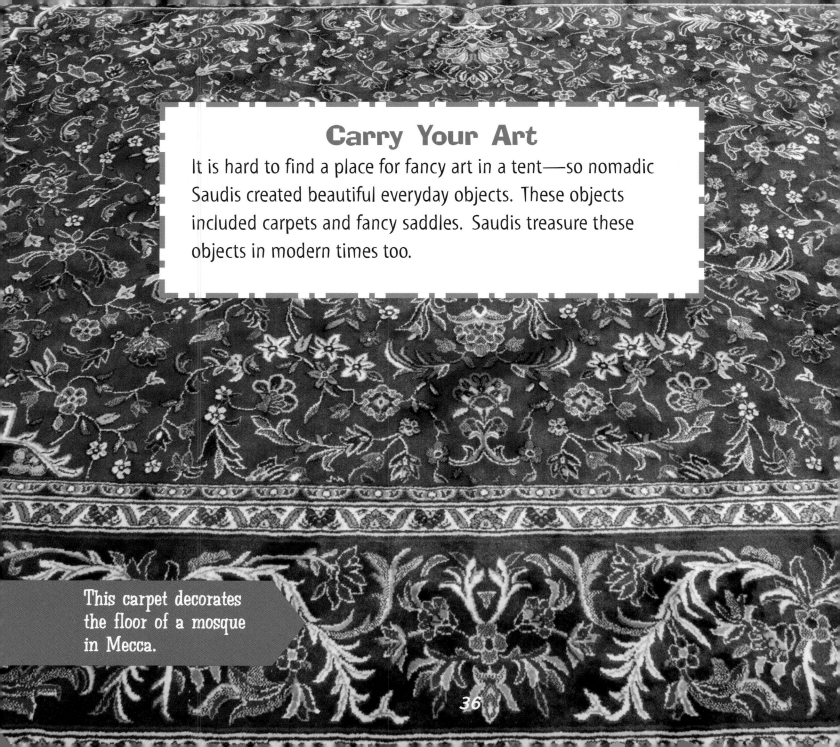

Carry Your Art

It is hard to find a place for fancy art in a tent—so nomadic Saudis created beautiful everyday objects. These objects included carpets and fancy saddles. Saudis treasure these objects in modern times too.

This carpet decorates the floor of a mosque in Mecca.

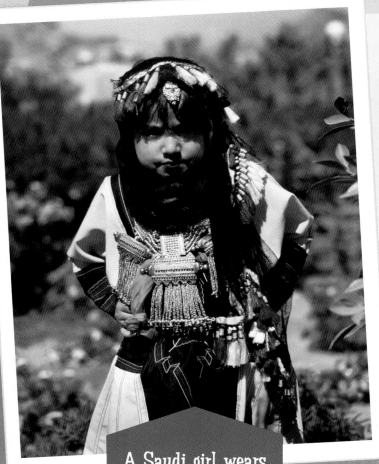

Many Saudis admire beautiful jewelry. Some Saudis wear five bracelets or rings. Five is considered a lucky number. Children like to wear bell-trimmed anklets and bracelets.

A Saudi girl wears jewelry trimmed with bells and colorful tassels.

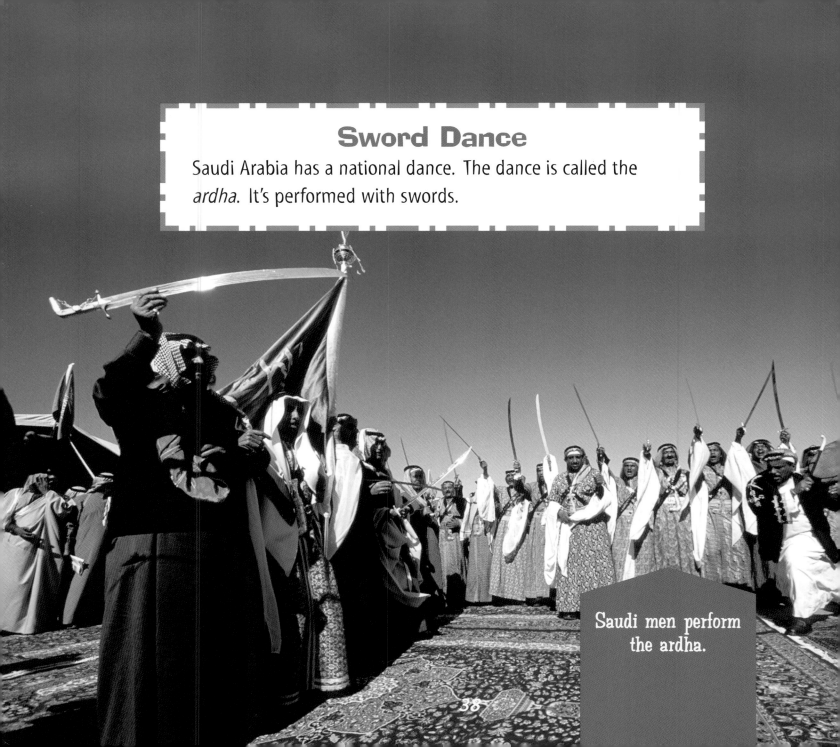

Sword Dance

Saudi Arabia has a national dance. The dance is called the *ardha*. It's performed with swords.

Saudi men perform the ardha.

The ardha is very exciting to watch. Men stand shoulder to shoulder in rows. They all face in the same direction.

In the center of the group, a poet sings. Drummers beat a rhythm. The men step and sway. They wave their swords in the air. The dance can be done with just a few people or with hundreds.

Drummers play for dancers performing the ardha.

Celebrate!

A three-day festival marks the end of Ramadan. Families go to mosques. Then they go home to exchange gifts and eat a feast. Many people wear new clothes. They also give gifts to the poor.

Boys dance and play drums to mark the end of Ramadan.

Another fun festival takes place in the spring. It's the Jenadriyah Heritage and Cultural Festival. Saudis celebrate their culture on this day.

Poets recite famous verses. People display many crafts. Dancers perform the ardha.

This boy has decorated his camel. A camel race kicks off the Jenadriyah Heritage and Cultural Festival.

Fun in Saudi Arabia

Falconry is a traditional Saudi Arabian pastime. This sport involves training falcons to hunt other birds. Saudi falcon trainers treat their falcons with great care.

This young man is training his falcon to hunt.

Children play soccer on a desert field. Soccer is the most popular team sport in Saudia Arabia.

Many Saudi families enjoy camping in the desert. They pack a picnic lunch to eat.

Campers nap in the hot afternoons. They stay awake at night, when it is cool.

THE FLAG OF SAUDI ARABIA

Saudi Arabia's flag is green and white. Green is an important color in Saudi Arabia. It is the color of Islam. It is also thought to be Muhammad's favorite color. Arabic words are in the center of the green flag. The words say, "There is no God but Allah, and Muhammad is his prophet." Below the words lies a sword. The sword shows that Saudis will fight to spread the Islamic faith.

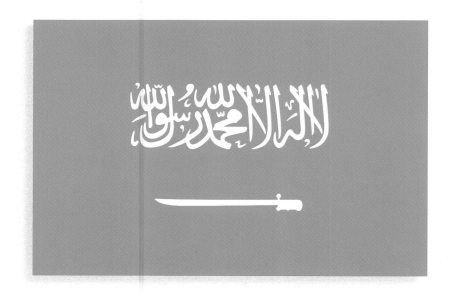